A TASTE OF

Drinks

A TASTE OF

Drinks

Sippable Recipes
in a Pint-Size Book

INSIGHT EDITIONS

SAN RAFAEL · LOS ANGELES · LONDON

Contents

DIETARY KEY   GF: Gluten-free   V+: Vegan
                      V: Vegetarian   V+*: Easily Made Vegan
                      V*: Easily Made Vegetarian

Introduction

Welcome to *A Taste of Disney: Drinks*, a selection of delectable libations inspired by beloved Disney films. From the refreshingly icy Cheshire Cat Grin and cooling Underworld Smoothies to the warming Pumpkin Spice Hot Cocoa and cozy Apple Cider Worth Melting For, you can mix up the perfect concoction to share with family and friends as you gather to watch your favorite Disney films. Each recipe is tailor-made for you to connect to a character or film you love. Enjoy!

Peddler's Disguise

Snow White and the Seven Dwarfs

When she discovers that Snow White is
still alive, the Queen heads to her dungeon
laboratory to devise a potion that will change
her appearance and allow her to get to
Snow White undetected. "Now, a formula to
transform my beauty into ugliness, change my
queenly raiment to a peddler's cloak," she says.
"Mummy dust, to make me old. To shroud my
clothes, the black of night. To age my voice, an
old hag's cackle. To whiten my hair, a scream
of fright! A blast of wind to fan my hate. A
thunderbolt to mix it well." The Queen's magic
potion turns her into an old peddler. This
concoction won't turn you into anyone else,
but it does make the house smell so good that
you might think there's magic in the air.

Peddler's Disguise

GF, V, V+ | Yield: 6 servings

8 cups fresh apple cider or unfiltered apple juice
2 cinnamon sticks
1 orange, sliced into thin wheels
4 whole cloves
1-inch piece fresh ginger

1. In a large saucepan over medium heat, combine the apple cider, cinnamon sticks, orange slices, cloves, and ginger. Bring to a simmer for 5 minutes.

2. Ladle into mugs, avoiding the solids in the pan. Garnish with the orange slices, if desired. Enjoy warm.

Black Forest
Hot Cocoa

Snow White and the Seven Dwarfs

The forest can be a dark, scary place—
especially when you're all alone. Inspired by
Snow White's night in the forest, this cup of
hot chocolate is sure to warm your bones
after a night spent in the woods!

Black Forest Hot Cocoa

GF, V | **Yield:** 4 servings

3 ounces good-quality bittersweet chocolate, chopped
⅓ cup plus 2 tablespoons granulated sugar, divided
2 cups whole milk, divided
¼ teaspoon almond extract
½ cup 100% cherry juice
¾ cup heavy whipping cream
Chocolate shavings
4 candied dark cherries (premium cocktail cherries)

SPECIALTY TOOLS
Piping bag with large star tip

1. In a medium saucepan, combine the chocolate, ⅓ cup sugar, and ½ cup of the milk. Cook, stirring constantly, over medium heat just until mixture comes to a boil. Stir in the remaining 1½ cups milk. Remove from heat. Stir in the almond extract and cherry juice.

2. In a medium bowl, beat the whipping cream with the remaining 2 tablespoons sugar until stiff peaks form. Spoon into a piping bag with a large star tip.

3. Ladle the chocolate mixture into 4 mugs. Pipe whipped cream on top of each mug. Sprinkle with chocolate shavings and top each with a cherry. Serve immediately.

Pumpkin Spice
Hot Cocoa

Cinderella

Oh, Cinderelly, Cinderelly! Cinderella's mouse friends sing about the many chores that Cinderella must do each day at the bidding of her stepmother and stepsisters. The friends, worried that Cinderella will have no time to sew a beautiful gown for the ball, stitch one as a gift. However, the jealous stepsisters rip the gown apart. Like Jaq and Gus Gus saving the day by helping Cinderella with her dress, pumpkin spice hot cocoa sets the world—or at least the day—to all things right for tea party guests.

Pumpkin Spice Hot Cocoa

GF, V* | **Yield:** 4 servings

⅓ cup cocoa powder
½ cup packed dark brown sugar
1 teaspoon pumpkin pie spice
Pinch salt
⅓ cup water
4 cups milk
Mini marshmallows, for garnish

1. In a large saucepan, combine the cocoa powder, dark brown sugar, pumpkin pie spice, salt, and the water. Set the heat to medium and bring to a boil, stirring constantly. Once the sugar is dissolved, stir in the milk and heat thoroughly but not to boiling. Remove the cocoa from heat and divide evenly among 4 mugs.

2. Garnish with mini marshmallows.

NOTE: This cocoa is vegetarian if marshmallows are omitted (or if using vegetarian marshmallows).

Growth Potion

Alice in Wonderland

Even in a most unusual world, it's important to remember that if one drinks too much from a particular type of bottle, its contents are certain to disagree with one sooner or later. Luckily, this Growth Potion is most agreeable—and particularly delicious! With its oh-so-lovely layers and its scintillating flavor of pineapple mixed with cherries and cream soda, this glittering beverage brings a sprinkle of magic to even the most humdrum of days.

Growth Potion

GF, V | **Yield:** 2 servings

1 cup pineapple juice
One 12-ounce can cream soda
Whipped cream
4 tablespoons syrup from bar cherries in syrup
2 bar cherries

1. Fill 2 tall glasses with ice. Split the pineapple juice between the glasses. Use a spoon to layer the cream soda over the juice; you might have extra soda.

2. Top with whipped cream, drizzle 2 tablespoons of cherry syrup over the whipped cream, and top with a cherry.

3. Serve immediately.

Cheshire Cat Grin

Alice in Wonderland

Nothing in Wonderland is quite as it seems, and that is most apparent with the mysterious Cheshire Cat, who has a tendency to leave his smile behind when he vanishes! This color-changing libation won't make you grow bigger or smaller, but it is sure to leave a grin on your face long after it's gone!

Cheshire Cat Grin

GF, V, V+ | **Yield:** 2 servings

SYRUP
1 cup water
1 cup raw (demerara) sugar
1 teaspoon butterfly pea flower powder

ICE CUBES
¼ cup lavender blossoms or other edible flowers
¾ cup fresh lemon juice, strained

SERVING
8 ounces (4 ounces per glass)
lemon-flavored sparkling water, chilled
1½ ounces fresh lemon juice
Lavender sprigs, for garnish

1. **To make the syrup:** In a small saucepan, heat the water and sugar over medium heat, stirring often, until the mixture begins to simmer and the sugar is dissolved. Remove from heat. Stir in the pea powder; cover and let steep for 20 minutes. Strain into a glass jar and cool completely.

2. **To make the ice cubes:** Sprinkle the lavender blossoms into enough ice cube trays to make 2 drinks (about 4 standard cubes). Pour the strained lemon juice over the blossoms. Freeze for 4 hours or overnight.

3. **To serve:** Place ¾ ounce of the blue syrup in each of two 8-ounce cocktail glasses. Add sparkling water to each glass. Do not stir. Add ¾ ounce lemon juice to each glass. Add 2 lemon ice cubes to each glass. Garnish with lavender sprigs.

4. Wait for the magic color change from blue to purple!

Tick-Tock Croc Drink

Peter Pan

If there's one thing Captain Hook fears, it's the crocodile! Luckily, he can always tell the croc is coming by the sound of a clock tick-tocking in its belly. One tick-tock and you'll be running too . . . to get another one of these delicious green beverages!

Tick-Tock Croc Drink

GF, V, V+ | **Yield:** 2 servings

JALAPEÑO SYRUP
½ cup raw (demerara) sugar
½ cup water
1 jalapeño, sliced (seeded if desired)

MINT SUGAR
¼ cup granulated sugar
¼ cup fresh mint leaves

SERVING
4 tablespoons Granny Smith green apple beverage syrup
Crushed ice
1 cup apple juice, chilled
One 7.2-ounce can club soda, chilled
2 lemon wedges
2 very thin green apple slices, for garnish, optional

1. **To make the jalapeño syrup:** In a small saucepan, combine the raw sugar, water, and jalapeño. Bring just to a simmer over medium heat, stirring frequently to dissolve the sugar. Remove from heat. Cover and let steep for 20 minutes. Strain into a glass jar; cool completely. Reserve jalapeño slices, if desired.

2. **To make the mint sugar:** In a small food processor or bullet-style blender, combine the granulated sugar and mint leaves. Process until the mint is ground and sugar is greenish in color. Right before serving the drink, spread the mint sugar onto a small plate or saucer.

3. **To serve:** Brush the rim of 2 margarita glasses with some of the jalapeño syrup (or the green apple syrup for less bite). Dip the glass rims into the mint sugar, getting as much sugar to stick as possible. Fill each glass half full with crushed ice. Pour 1 tablespoon jalapeño syrup and 2 tablespoons Granny Smith apple syrup into each glass. Top with apple juice and club soda. Squeeze lemon wedges into each drink and drop into the glasses.

4. If desired, garnish each drink with a candied jalapeño slice and very thin apple slice.

Toast to the Future Sparkling Punch

Sleeping Beauty

Once a kiss from Aurora's true love, Prince Phillip, lifts Maleficent's evil curse, the kingdom awakens to celebrate. This colorful, flavorful, sparkling punch combines strawberry slush, ginger ale, and sherbet as the ideal drink to celebrate a happy ending and toast to the future.

Toast to the Future Sparkling Punch

GF, V | **Yield:** 4 servings

2 cups frozen strawberries, partially defrosted
4 cups cold ginger ale
1 cup rainbow sherbet

1. In a food processor or blender, process the strawberries until smooth (strawberries may appear slushy). Divide the processed strawberries evenly among four 1-pint glasses. Slowly pour 1 cup of the ginger ale into each glass, pausing when bubbles rise.

2. Drop a ¼-cup scoop of sherbet into each glass. Serve with straws. Advise guests to stir gently before drinking to combine the flavors.

Mermaid's Kiss

The Little Mermaid

Ariel longs to be with Eric and with the world above, so much so that she has Ursula the sea witch turn her human. But to stay human, she needs to get Eric to kiss her before her three days are up. Unfortunately, that isn't as easy as it seems without her voice. But making this passion-fruit-filled drink *is* easy!

Mermaid's Kiss

GF, V, V+ | **Yield:** 2 servings

1 cup frozen passion fruit cubes, thawed
2 lime wedges (¼ lime)
2 tablespoons granulated sugar
Crushed ice
4 tablespoons strawberry beverage syrup
One 12-ounce can hibiscus- or guava-flavored
sparkling water, chilled
2 pink hibiscus flowers, for garnish

1. Place the passion fruit cubes in a small bowl. Add the lime wedges and sugar. Muddle the mixture with a wooden spoon to release the lime juice and break up the passion fruit pulp.

2. Fill 2 tall 12-ounce cocktail glasses half full of crushed ice. Pour 2 tablespoons strawberry beverage syrup in each glass and divide the sparkling water between the 2 glasses.

3. Spoon the passion fruit mixture, including lime wedges, over the top of each glass. Garnish each glass with a hibiscus flower.

Flounder Striped Smoothie

The Little Mermaid

Ariel's best friend, Flounder, has beautifully vibrant yellow and blue stripes. This delicious smoothie pays tribute to his stripes by alternating layers of mango and blueberries! It might sound complicated to make a layered smoothie, but it's actually surprisingly quick. It takes only 10 minutes in the freezer for each layer of this smoothie to thicken enough for the back-and-forth pouring method. Even better, you get to drink a big cup of delicious blueberries and mango.

Flounder Striped Smoothie

GF, V, V+* | **Yield:** 2 servings

¾ cup frozen blueberries, plus more for garnish, optional
1 cup frozen banana chunks or slices, divided
⅔ cup yogurt, divided
1 cup apple juice, divided
6 ice cubes, divided
¾ cup frozen mango chunks, plus more for garnish, optional

NOTE: For the yogurt in this recipe, any will work: plain or flavored, Greek or regular, dairy or plant-based.

1. To make the blueberry layer, in a blender combine the blueberries and half each of the banana, yogurt, apple juice, and ice. Blend on high until smooth, then pour into a large glass and place in the freezer. Rinse out the blender.

2. To make the mango layer, in the blender combine the mango and the remaining half each of the banana, yogurt, apple juice, and ice. Blend on high until smooth, then pour into a large glass and place in the freezer. Freeze for 10 minutes.

3. To assemble the smoothie, set out 2 tall glasses. Take the smoothies out of the freezer and stir briefly to break up any ice chunks that may have formed. Pour 1 to 2 inches of blueberry smoothie into each glass, then pour 1 to 2 inches of mango smoothie on top of that. If they begin to meld together, pour each layer over the upturned bowl of a spoon into the cup. Continue until each glass is full and each of the smoothie layers has been used up. If desired, garnish with additional mango chunks and blueberries.

Enchanted Rosewater Lemonade

Beauty and the Beast

The Beast has been cursed to find true love before the last petal falls from his enchanted rose. If he doesn't succeed, the beautiful rose, left by the enchantress, will fade, and as a consequence, the Beast and his friends will remain as they are. In this lemonade, floral rosewater is a reminder of the Beast's journey to understand love.

Enchanted Rosewater Lemonade

GF, V, V+ | **Yield:** 4 servings

SIMPLE SYRUP
1 cup water
1 cup granulated sugar
1 tablespoon rosewater

LEMONADE
3 cups water
Juice of 4 lemons (about ¾ cup)
Ice, for serving
Fresh mint, for garnish

1. **To make the simple syrup:** In a small saucepan combine the water, sugar, and rosewater. Heat and stir over medium heat until the sugar is dissolved, 2 to 3 minutes. Remove from heat.

2. **To make the lemonade:** Combine the water and lemon juice in a large pitcher. Stir in the simple syrup to combine. Chill until ready to serve. To serve, pour over ice and garnish with fresh mint.

Sour Cherry Smoothies

Aladdin

Fresh cherries can be hard to come by out of season if you aren't somewhere with a warm climate, but tart cherry juice and frozen cherries make this smoothie into something you can enjoy at any time of year. The tart juice-and-fruit combo adds an adventurous flair that bursts with flavor . . . just like Jasmine's bursting curiosity to explore her own kingdom! This easy on-the-go breakfast includes probiotic kefir, a beverage full of protein to fuel Jasmine on her travels.

Sour Cherry Smoothies

GF, V | **Yield:** 1 large serving

½ cup tart cherry juice

1 cup plain kefir

1 cup frozen cherries

½ cup frozen banana chunks or slices,
plus more slices for garnish, optional

1 teaspoon honey

2 ice cubes

Edible flowers, optional

1. In a blender, combine the cherry juice, kefir, cherries, banana, honey, and ice cubes; blend until smooth. (This should take about 30 seconds in a high-power blender, or about 1 minute in a standard blender.)

2. Garnish with banana slices and edible flowers, if desired.

> **NOTE:** Because dairy kefir has much more protein than plant-based, it's the recommended option in this recipe.

Watermelon Sparkler

Aladdin

This is a drink that Aladdin's friend Abu would surely want to get his hands on! And even though he's not a big fan of sharing food, this sparkler is so good that Abu would want to share it with Aladdin! Watermelon is such a wonderfully sweet fruit that you can make a sparkling drink of it with no additional sweetener needed. Because you'll be blending the whole fruit into the beverage, you won't lose any of its healthful fiber, either. This sparkler is refreshing on a summer day, but can bring summer vibes into any season if fresh watermelon is available near you.

If you don't have crushed ice on hand, place several ice cubes in a freezer-strength resealable plastic bag, and use a rolling pin or meat mallet to smash the ice into small pieces.

Watermelon Sparkler

GF, V, V+ | **Yield:** 4 servings

4 cups cubed fresh watermelon,
seeds removed if not seedless
½ teaspoon ground ginger
1 tablespoon lime juice
4 cups crushed ice
Sparkling water
Lime wedge or wheel, for garnish, optional
Slice of watermelon, for garnish, optional

1. In a blender combine the watermelon, ginger, and lime juice, and blend on high until the mixture looks very smooth.

2. Pour the watermelon juice into 4 large glasses. Add crushed ice to the glasses and stir briefly. Top with sparkling water.

3. If desired, garnish with a lime wedge, lime wheel, or slice of watermelon.

Underworld Smoothies

Hercules

"If there's one god you don't want to get steamed up, it's Hades, 'cause he had an evil plan," the Muses sing. "He ran the underworld, but thought the dead were dull and uncouth. He was as mean as he was ruthless, and that's the gospel truth." But Hades does get steamed up all the time, especially when his evil plans to defeat Hercules are thwarted.

This healthy breakfast smoothie plays on Hades's two moods: When he's calm, he has blue flames for hair; when he's angry, those flames turn red. Mix each recipe separately, then pour both in the same glass to get a true representation of Hades's feelings.

Underworld Smoothies

GF, V | **Yield:** 2 servings

CALM BLUE SMOOTHIE
1 cup frozen blueberries
½ cup frozen blackberries
¼ cup plain Greek yogurt
½ cup grape, blueberry, or blackberry juice
1 cup ice

ANGRY RED SMOOTHIE
1 cup frozen strawberries
½ cup frozen raspberries
¼ cup plain Greek yogurt
½ cup strawberry, cranberry, or beet juice
1 cup ice

1. **To make the calm blue smoothie:** Put the blueberries, blackberries, Greek yogurt, grape (or alternate) juice, and ice in a blender, and blend until combined. Pour into a measuring cup with a pouring lip and set aside.

2. **To make the angry red smoothie:** Put the strawberries, raspberries, Greek yogurt, strawberry (or alternate) juice, and ice in a blender, and blend until combined.

3. **To serve:** Holding a vessel in each hand, pour half the two smoothies into a drinking glass at the same time, then repeat with a second glass. Enjoy cold.

NOTE: Fruits like blueberries contain high levels of antioxidants. Antioxidants can help protect your body against free radicals, which can contribute to diseases.

Iced Orange Green Tea

Mulan

When Mulan meets with the matchmaker, she tells Mulan that she needs to exhibit dignity, refinement, and poise as she pours tea to please her future in-laws. The visit doesn't go well and the matchmaker is not impressed. Fortunately, Mulan finds her own path that brings her family honor. This refreshing iced tea with orange flavor is made with green tea. Though it's inspired by Mulan's unsuccessful experience with the matchmaker, this iced tea is definitely a success.

Iced Orange Green Tea

GF, V | **Yield:** 4 servings

4 green tea teabags
4 cups boiling water
2 tablespoons honey
Juice of 2 oranges (about 1 cup)
1 orange, cut into thin slices (ends discarded)
Ice, for serving
Fresh mint, for garnish

1. Place the teabags into a large measuring cup or 4-cup heat-safe container. Add the boiling water and stir in the honey. Let steep, uncovered, for 10 minutes. Remove the teabags, pressing them with a spoon against the side of the container to extract all the green tea. Let cool at least 20 minutes.

2. In a pitcher, stir together the green tea and orange juice. Add the orange slices. Chill until ready to serve; serve over ice, garnished with fresh mint.

The Green Flash

Lilo & Stitch

Lilo and Stitch love watching the sunset from the comfort of their hammock. The mysterious green light that flashes as the sun sets reminds them of when Stitch first landed in Hawai'i. This green drink is for sure out of this world!

The Green Flash

GF, V, V+ | **Yield:** 2 to 4

¼ cup fresh lemon juice
1 cup pineapple juice
½ cup ginger syrup
2 to 3 ounces green apple soda

SPECIAL SUPPLIES
Transparent tiki glass (or something you can
easily see through), optional
Silly straw, optional

1. Pour the lemon juice, pineapple juice, ginger syrup, and
   green apple soda into the glass with ice and stir slightly.

2. To garnish, place a silly straw in each glass, if desired.

NOTE: Place a glow cube switched to a non-pulsing
white light color for an out-of-this world light show in
your drink.

Lū'au Blue Hawaiian Drink

Lilo & Stitch

Lilo spends a lot of time at the lū'au where Nani works. Although she often wishes she could be somewhere else, Lilo does enjoy getting the lū'au's tasty nonalcoholic drinks—especially when they come with an umbrella!

Lūʻau Blue Hawaiian Drink

GF, V, V+ | **Yield:** 4 servings

GINGER-LIME SYRUP
½ cup raw (demerara) sugar
½ cup water
3 slices fresh gingerroot
1 teaspoon lime zest

DRINK
8 ounces 100% pineapple juice, chilled
8 ounces coconut water chilled
Two 12-ounce cans unsweetened lemon-
or lime-flavored sparkling water, chilled
Several teaspoons butterfly pea flower extract
Ice cubes

SERVING
Pineapple wedges
Paper umbrellas
Edible mini orchid flowers

1. **To make the ginger-lime syrup:** In a small saucepan, combine the sugar, water, gingerroot, and lime zest. Bring to a boil over medium-high heat. Remove from heat; cover and let steep for 10 minutes. Remove the ginger slices.

2. **To make the drink:** In a pitcher, combine the ginger-lime syrup, pineapple juice, coconut water, and sparkling water. Add enough pea flower extract to make desired color.

3. Serve in tall cocktail glasses over ice. Garnish with pineapple wedges, paper umbrellas, and orchid flowers.

Mardi Gras Smoothie

The Princess and the Frog

When Tiana and Naveen find their way back to New Orleans, they're caught up in the colorful Mardi Gras parade. Inspired by the bright colors of Mardi Gras, this smoothie is topped with colorful sprinkles. The smoothie ingredients are a take on King Cake, a traditional dessert served during Mardi Gras.

Mardi Gras Smoothie

GF, V | **Yield:** 4 servings

2 cups milk
2 cups vanilla yogurt
2 tablespoons light brown sugar
⅔ cup pecans
½ cup golden raisins
Sanding sugar in purple, green, and gold

1. In a blender, combine the milk, yogurt, brown sugar, pecans, and raisins. Blend thoroughly until the pecans and raisins are itty-bitty pieces. Divide among 4 glasses. Decorate each with purple, green, and gold sugars, then serve.

Sundrop Flower Sipper

Tangled

Rapunzel's hair may be magical, but that magic came from a single drop of sunlight that fell to the ground and grew into a beautiful golden flower. This delightful yellow drink—topped with an edible yellow flower—celebrates that magical drop of sunlight!

Sundrop Flower Sipper

GF, V, V+ | **Yield:** 2 servings

GINGER-BASIL SYRUP
½ cup water
¼ cup raw (demerara) or granulated sugar
2 thin slices fresh ginger root
4 large basil leaves

DRINK
Two 6-ounce cans 100% pineapple juice, chilled
Ice cubes
2 lime wedges
One 12-ounce can or bottle ginger beer, chilled (see note)

SERVING
2 yellow edible nasturtium blossoms

1. **To make the ginger-basil syrup:** In a small saucepan, combine the water and sugar over medium heat. Heat, stirring constantly, until the sugar is dissolved. Remove from heat and stir in the ginger root and basil. Let steep for 10 minutes. Strain the syrup into a glass jar and cool completely.

2. **To make the drink:** In a small pitcher, combine the ginger-basil syrup and pineapple juice. Place 2 large ice cubes in each of 2 cocktail glasses. Squeeze a lime wedge over each glass and drop into the glasses. Pour the pineapple mixture over the ice. Pour the ginger beer into the glasses and garnish with nasturtium blossoms.

NOTE: Ginger beer is non-alcoholic.

Daydreaming Fruit Tea

Tangled

While growing up locked in the tower, Rapunzel becomes creative in the kitchen— baking pies, dozens of cookies, and other sweet treats. Still, even as she experiments, she wonders when her real life will begin. This flavor-bending combination of fresh fruit juice and fragrant green tea would likely set Rapunzel to dreaming beyond the tower walls.

Daydreaming Fruit Tea

GF, V, V+ | **Yield:** 6 servings

2 cups watermelon
1 cup strawberries, plus more for garnish
½ cup blueberries
3 cups water, divided
3 green tea teabags

1. In a blender, combine the watermelon, the 1 cup strawberries, and the blueberries, and blend until smooth. Strain the mixture through a fine-mesh sieve into a pitcher, removing fruit solids. Stir in 1 cup of the water.

2. In a small pot, heat the remaining 2 cups water to boiling. Remove from heat and submerge the teabags in the hot water. Steep for 10 minutes, uncovered. Remove the teabags, then pour the tea into the punch. Stir to combine. Chill until ready to serve, or serve immediately over ice, garnished with fresh whole strawberries.

Apple Cider Worth Melting For

Frozen

Olaf knows that some people are worth melting for. The loyal snowman risks his own life to help the freezing Anna, building a fire—and learning what warmth feels like!—to ensure she holds on. This spicy apple cider invokes the flavors of the North to create a beverage that could warm even the coldest heart. With apples, lingonberry, cinnamon, and cardamom, Apple Cider Worth Melting For will bring to mind Olaf's wise words: "So this is heat. I love it!"

Apple Cider Worth Melting For

GF, V, V+* | **Yield:** 4 servings

4 cups apple juice or apple cider
¼ cup lingonberry preserves
2 cinnamon sticks, plus more for serving
4 cardamom pods
1 large strip of orange peel
4 whole cloves
4 whole allspice berries
1 star anise, plus more for serving
Sugar or honey, to taste, optional
2 tablespoons dried unsweetened cranberries
Cinnamon sticks, for serving, optional

NOTE: If you use sugar instead of honey, this cider will be vegan.

1. In a medium saucepan over medium heat, combine the apple juice or cider, lingonberry preserves, cinnamon sticks, cardamom pods, orange peel, cloves, allspice berries, and star anise. Bring to a gentle simmer, then lower to low heat and simmer for about 15 minutes, adjusting heat as needed. Strain out the spices and solids, reserving the liquid in a jar.

2. Taste and add a little sugar or honey if you want a sweeter cider.

3. Divide between 4 mugs, add dried cranberries to each, and garnish with additional cinnamon sticks or star anise, if desired.

Honey-Lemon Bees Knees

Big Hero 6

Honey Lemon is a brave and loyal member of Big Hero 6. A self-proclaimed chemistry whiz, she can whip up chemballs for any occasion. Luckily, when she's not fighting bad guys, Honey Lemon is as sweet as her name. She's always looking on the bright side and ready for anything. You will be, too, after a taste of this honey-based beverage!

Honey-Lemon Bees Knees

GF, V | **Yield:** 1 serving (enough syrup for 4 drinks)

HONEY SYRUP
¼ cup honey
¼ cup boiling water
1 small sprig rosemary

DRINK
Ice
2 ounces 100% pineapple juice
Freshly squeezed lemon juice
4 ounces sparkling water, chilled
Rosemary sprig

1. **To make the honey syrup:** In a small glass measuring cup, combine the honey and boiling water. Add the rosemary sprig. Let stand for 15 minutes. Remove the rosemary sprig and discard.

2. **To make the drink:** Fill a cocktail shaker with ice. Add 1 ounce of the honey syrup, the pineapple juice, and a splash of lemon juice. Shake well; strain into a coupe glass. Pour in the sparkling water. Garnish with a rosemary sprig.

Coconut-Mango Coolers

Moana

Feel as daring as Moana while sipping on refreshing coconut-mango coolers during a tea party. Combine refreshing coconut water with sweet mango, tart lime, and bubbly club soda for a delightful drink.

Coconut-Mango Coolers

GF, V, V+ | **Yield:** 4 servings

2 cups coconut water
Juice of 1 lime
2 cups frozen mango
1 cup club soda, divided
Lime slices, halved, for garnish

1. In a blender, combine coconut water, lime juice, and frozen mango chunks. Blend until smooth. Divide blended mixture among 4 large beverage glasses. Top each with ¼ cup club soda. Serve immediately, garnished with lime slices.

Hibiscus Flower Water

Coco

The drink stands in Coco's La Plaza Santa Cecilia sell these fruity refreshers from large clear jugs, with all their vibrant colors on full display. They are the perfect refresher to have when you're watching the mariachi play in the talent contest (just don't tell Abuelita that you were there).

Hibiscus Flower Water

GF, V, V+ | **Yield:** 4 servings

1½ cups dried hibiscus flowers
⅔ cup sugar
Juice of 1 lime (about 1 tablespoon)

1. Rinse the dried hibiscus flowers under cold water in a strainer, to remove all dust and grit.

2. In a medium pot over high heat, bring 2 quarts (8 cups) of water to a boil. Add the rinsed flowers and sugar, stirring to dissolve the sugar; then turn off the heat and let steep for 30 minutes. When cooled to room temperature, the flowers will fall to the bottom of the pot.

3. Strain the hibiscus water into a pitcher, and stir in the lime juice. Refrigerate the drink until it is cold. Serve over ice, adjusting the sugar or lime juice to suit your taste.

Rice and Almond Milk with Cinnamon

Coco

Rice and almonds give this classic agua a satisfyingly creamy and frothy texture. Spiked with sweet and floral Mexican cinnamon and a splash of vanilla, it's a perfect companion to spicier foods that may have been served at Santa Cecilia's very own Tortillería in the film. In some parts of Mexico, this drink, called horchata, is topped with chopped summer fruits and nuts.

Rice and Almond Milk with Cinnamon

GF, V, V+ | **Yield:** 6 servings

1 cup uncooked long-grain white rice
1 cup raw almonds
One 3-inch Mexican cinnamon stick
½ teaspoon kosher salt
3 cups boiling water, plus 3 cups cold water, divided
⅓ to ½ cup sugar
1 teaspoon vanilla extract

1. To a heatproof container, add the rice, almonds, cinnamon stick, salt, and 3 cups of boiling water. Leave uncovered at room temperature for at least 2 hours, but preferably overnight. The longer the rice mixture sits, the deeper the flavor will be.

2. After the rice has softened, add the entire mixture to a blender along with 3 cups of cold water, the sugar, and the vanilla. Blend the mixture on the blender's highest setting for at least 2 minutes until it is very smooth.

3. Pass the blended rice mixture through a fine-mesh strainer or cheesecloth into a pitcher. Serve well chilled over ice.

Passion Fruit Butterfly Bliss

Encanto

A yellow butterfly appeared in Bruno's vision, leading the way to a bright future for Mirabel and Alma's family, whom they love and protect passionately.

The bliss and profound joy of that moment must be celebrated! We present you with a fruit as mystic and full of passion as the Amazon Rainforest itself. Passion fruit, also known as maracuyá or parcha in some Latin American countries, is a versatile tropical fruit that can be used for a variety of dishes, including cold juice, sweet sorbets, smoothies, sauces, jellies, and desserts like mousse and cheesecake.

Passion Fruit Butterfly Bliss

GF, V, V+* | **Yield:** 2 servings

¼ cup passion fruit pulp (1 large passion fruit)
2 tablespoons sugar
3 cups water or 2 cups milk and 1 cup water
1 cup crushed ice

1. In a blender, place the passion fruit pulp. Blend for 3 seconds, pass through a sieve, and place the remaining liquid back into the blender. Discard the seeds. Add the sugar, water or milk, and ice, and blend to a smoothie. Pour into 2 glasses and serve.

> **NOTE:** This same recipe works for the curuba fruit. This recipe is dairy-free and vegan if the milk is omitted.

Fruity Fiesta Medley

Encanto

The town in Encanto is a colorful display of vibrant details. In this Fruity Fiesta Medley, inspired by a drink called salpicón, when you combine the assorted flavors and textures of tropical fruits, diced small, and packed in their own juicy sweetness, you'll feel as if you're tasting a rainbow. You can serve this drink in individual cups for a naturally refreshing party at home. It would surely become a favorite among the Madrigal kids, especially if topped with a scoop of vanilla ice cream.

Fruity Fiesta Medley

GF, V, V+* | **Yield:** 8 to 10 servings

3 cups finely diced papaya (about 1 medium,
or 3 Hawaiian papayas) or 3 cups finely diced watermelon
(about ½ watermelon)
1 teaspoon sugar, optional
1 teaspoon lemon juice, optional
2 cups finely diced pineapple (about ½ pineapple)
2 cups finely diced mango
2 bananas, chopped
8 to 10 small scoops vanilla ice cream, optional

1. In a blender, blend 2 cups of the papaya or watermelon
   and ½ cup water into a juice consistency. Taste for
   sweetness and add the optional sugar, if desired. When
   using papaya for the juice, add the lemon juice.

2. In a large bowl, place the remaining papaya and/or
   watermelon, the pineapple, and mango. Pour the
   papaya juice over the fruit, add the banana, and mix.
   Serve cold with or without ice cream. Keep refrigerated.

NOTE: Two cups fresh orange juice can be used
instead of papaya juice. This recipe is vegan if served
without ice cream.

FIND MORE RECIPES FROM Disney

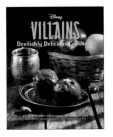

INSIGHT
EDITIONS

PO Box 3088
San Rafael, CA 94912
www.insighteditions.com

Find us on Facebook:
www.facebook.com/InsightEditions

Follow us on Instagram:
@insighteditions

ISBN: 979-8-88663-700-7

Publisher: Raoul Goff
Group Publisher & SVP: Vanessa Lopez
VP, Creative: Chrissy Kwasnik
VP, Manufacturing: Alix Nicholaeff
Publishing Director: Paul Ruditis
Art Director: Stuart Smith
Senior Designer: Judy Wiatrek Trum
Editor: Jennifer Pellman
Executive Project Editor: Maria Spano
Production Associate: Deena Hashem
Senior Production Manager, Subsidiary Rights:
Lina s Palma Temena

ROOTS of PEACE · REPLANTED PAPER

Insight Editions, in association with Roots of Peace, will
plant two trees for each tree used in the manufacturing of
this book. Roots of Peace is an internationally renowned
humanitarian organization dedicated to eradicating land
mines worldwide and converting war-torn lands into
productive farms and wildlife habitats. Roots of Peace will
plant two million fruit and nut trees in Afghanistan and
provide farmers there with the skills and support necessary
for sustainable land use.

Manufactured in China by Insight Editions
10 9 8 7 6 5 4 3 2 1

Recipe Sources

Pages 8, 56 . . . . *Disney Villains: Devilishly Delicious Cookbook*
by Julie Tremaine

Pages 12, 24, 28, 36, 68, 76, 88 . . *Disney: Cooking with Magic* by Lisa Kingsley, Jennifer Peterson,
and Brooke Vitale

Pages 16, 32, 44, 60, 72, 80, 92 . . *Disney Princess Tea Parties Cookbook* by Sarah Walker Caron

Page 20 . . . . *Alice in Wonderland: The Official Cookbook* by Elena P. Craig
and S. T. Bende

Pages 40, 48, 52 . . . . *Disney Princess: Healthy Treats* by Ariane Resnick

Page 64 . . . . *Lilo and Stitch: The Official Cookbook* by Tim Rita

Page 84 . . . . *Disney Frozen: The Official Cookbook* by Daytona Danielsen
and S. T. Bende

Pages 96, 100 . . . . *Coco: The Official Cookbook* by Gino Garcia

Pages 104, 108 . . . . *Encanto: The Official Cookbook* by Patricia McCausland-
Gallo and Susana Illera Martínez